MONEY IS NOT YOUR LANDLORD, MONEY IS YOUR ROOMMATE

KEENAN WILLIAMS

Copyright © 2022 by Keenan Williams in partnership with Build Your Own Book Publishing LLC

Without limiting the rights under copyright reserved above, no part of this publication may be reproduced, stored in or introduced into a retrieval system, or transmitted, in any form, or by any means (electronic, mechanical, photocopying, recording, or otherwise), without the prior written permission of both the copyright owner and the publisher of the book. www.buildyourownbooks.com

ISBN: 9781513693637

Edited & Formatted by Lattifa Bryant,
Build Your Own Book Publishing LLC
Cover Design By: Lattifa Bryant

Manufactured in the United States of America

Follow the Publisher!
IG: @TheAuthorQueen
Email: hello@authorqueen.com

Connect with the author

Instagram: Papuchulo_dreaded
Website: www.nextbracket4u.com

DEDICATION

I dedicate this book to people who want a better understanding of money. I want you to imagine what life would be like if you could quit your 9 to 5 job, invest in yourself, and find a new path.

After today, you can stop allowing money to control your life. Inside, I will teach you how to make money work for you, instead of against you. Money is NOT Your Landlord, Money is Your Roommate.

Money is not someone who rules you. Money lives with you, and money cares about you. Learn how to put money where it belongs by joining my new program today at www.nextbracket4u.com.

TABLE OF CONTENTS

Foreword 1

Introduction 3

1. It's Time to Put Money in its Place 9

2. Stop Hustling Backwards 35

3. The Trifecta Combo 59

4. Hustle to the Next Bracket 69

5. Never Let Your Roommates Come Empty-Handed 83

6. Avoid Eviction 91

7. Market to Your First Million 105

8. Ready, Set, Launch! 111

FOREWORD

A million dollars in ten months sounds unrealistic. That's what I thought a year ago when I was working 60 plus hours a week on 12-hour shifts. I was a single, divorced mother of an autistic son, exhausted, lonely, depressed, and going through the motions. I did not have enough time to do what my son wanted to do or enough money to do what I wanted to do. I was desperately looking and praying for a change and then I found Keenan. I joined his program, watched the videos, and ate every bread crumb he put down. Under his direction, I got my website, logo, products, , and launched my business in two months. In one week, I doubled my investment and sold out.

Ten months in, I hit a million and the rest is history! I was able to walk away from my 6-figure job, spend more time with my son, and be my own boss. I even bought my dream car. Now, I am helping my family do the same! The need for money and time is now a thing of my past. It was simple but it wasn't easy. However, in order to have something different, you have to do something different. I am forever grateful that I took a leap of faith and joined Keenan's program.

Life is up from here!

Latonya Morris

INTRODUCTION:

No matter where you stand in your money journey, this book is for you. For the past couple of years, I have been known as a millionaire mentor, but if you would have met me back in 2018, you would have met a man who worshiped money at its feet. I worked 24/7 for money, and it took me years to realize that money worshipping is a type of money disorder.

After spending years worshipping money like some sort of lost God, I learned that I do not owe money ANYTHING. Money instead owes ME everything. I spent years trying to get out of my financial mess. As soon as I learned how to truly put money in its place, I became a self-made millionaire with only 300 bucks.

If you have ever wondered how to stop worshiping money and start living the life you desire, this book will show you the way.

Tired of being a slave to money? Sick of letting it rule our life? Well, the good news is that you can change that.

"I want to be wealthy" is a common goal, but very few people ever actually reach their financial goals. Why?

Because they don't have the right system in place to help them get there.

I've been where you are now. I've struggled, and I've found success — and I'm here to show you how to do the same. The book in your hands reveals methods that I have successfully used to generate over 8-figures for myself and several of my students. Filled with valuable strategies and straight-no-chaser advice, you will learn how to put money in its rightful place once and for all. I have laid out the foundation to help you clean up any financial situation—no matter what state it's currently in—and build a total money makeover plan specifically for YOU.

If you've ever found yourself wondering, "Why is money so bad?" or, "What's wrong with me that I can't stop thinking about money all the time?" then let me introduce to you something good: Money is your roommate. Money is here to help you live the life you want. From this day forward, money should be viewed as a roommate or tool that is here to help you afford the life you desire.

If that doesn't immediately put things into perspective, imagine being stuck in a tiny room with someone who never shuts up about the most random things.

Money's just like that.

It won't shut up about how it's going to make you happier and more successful than anyone else in the world—and it won't stop bothering you until you talk back.

If you learn how money works, then you'll be able to put it in its place—and get the life you deserve. **You do not have to dread or fear money any longer, because** money is here to meet you halfway.

I used to think money was the landlord—until I realized that I'm the one who's really in charge.

When you look at your bank account, do you feel like you're going to throw up? Do you worry about money even when there's nothing to worry about? Do you feel like your hard work never pays off?

I felt like that for years. After years of hustling backwards, it finally hit me: money is an inanimate object. It doesn't have feelings or opinions or desires. Money isn't trying to control me.

Money is my roommate. And if my roommate were trying to change ME, that would be ridiculous!

Why should it be any different with money?

Now I understand how money works—and how it fits into my life. My financial money anxiety is gone, and I've learned how to make my money work FOR me instead of against me.

If you're ready to stop letting the fear of money, misuse of money, and anxiety rule your life, then this book is for YOU!

In it, we'll cover everything from the ins and outs of budgeting to new ways to make money work for you.

Ready to put money in its place? Let's get started!

CHAPTER 1:
IT'S TIME TO PUT MONEY IN ITS PLACE

Money is a powerful tool, and it can be used to help you achieve your goals. However, if you are not careful with how you view and use money, your financial situation will gradually worsen over time.

If you want to win with money, you need to know how to put money in its proper place. What we believe about money often determines how we use it.

Money is your roommate and your partner, and it is here to help you strengthen and grow your life.

I want you to know that money is NOT your Landlord. Money does not rule you. Money should not be dreaded, feared, or worshipped. Money is a tool used to help you achieve your goals.

Money is just a roommate that is here to help you finance the life you desire. Money is here to support you. Money is here for you - you are not here for money.

Money is here to help you get through the day. You do not depend on money - money depends on you.

Money is supposed to provide comfort for you, but you must do your part to prepare for your new roommate.

Let's review a few ways that you can prepare to make room for your new roommate: money.

Take Out the Trash:

Start putting money in its place by taking out trash spending habits. Clean up your financial home so that you can make room for more money to come in. Stop throwing away money on useless things like impulse buying and paying excessive or unnecessary interest rates.

You know what I am talking about: the bills that have been piling up for weeks or months...that pile of debt that you keep avoiding, and those dirty spending habits such as that credit card statement with more interest charges than purchases.

These are all examples of how we waste our hard-earned cash by buying things we do not need and letting debt sit around until it begins to stink. Take out those bad spending habits and say goodbye to spending money in trash ways.

Tidy up!

Get your trash bag ready!

Clean Up Your Shared Spaces:

Be willing to let go of what is standing in your way of having money as your roommate. Keeping your financial space clean means that you will be able to see the opportunities for wealth and abundance when they show up, instead of having them pass by because there is too much clutter in your mind and your life.

You've probably heard the saying: "You can't climb a mountain if your arms are full of rocks." Well, the same is true of your money. You can't make room for wealth if your mind is cluttered with negative thoughts and your finances are full of debt.

That's why decluttering—both your mind and your finances—is a vital step to getting on the right track toward financial stability.

Let's take care of that mental clutter.

Many of us were taught limiting beliefs about money from our childhood, but these thoughts only hold us back. Begin challenging and changing those beliefs and replace ingrained bad thoughts about money with positive money mantras when you begin to work with your money.

Reciting positive money mantras will help you change your thought process.

Some positive money mantras include:

"I attract money easily and effortlessly."

"Money flows freely into my life, and Money is here to stay."

"I release all limiting beliefs about money."

"I am finding new ways to attract more money."

"I am worthy of a positive overflow of money."

"I always have more than enough money in my life."

"I naturally attract wealth. I am financially free."

"My income exceeds my expenses. My financial cup runneth over."

Instead of focusing on what you don't have or what you can't do, focus on what you DO have, whether that's small or large amounts of money saved up, a good credit score, or even just a solid plan for how you're going to get where you want to be financially.

Use these money mantras to clear out all the negative thoughts around money and wealth so they don't come back to haunt you later. A simple way to do this is by writing down all those negative beliefs about money in a journal or on a piece of paper (or even in a separate notebook), and then ripping them up into tiny pieces and physically throwing those bad thoughts away.

Decluttering your mind and your finances will make room for new wealth. You cannot change your financial habits if you do not first change your mind.

Unclutter Your Mind with These 3 Budgeting Tips

One of the most important ways to stay on top of your finances is to take care of the mental clutter that clouds your ability to think clearly about money. Use the following three tips to improve your money mindset and learn how to budget.

1. Get in the habit of living within your means. If you don't have the money for something, don't buy it. You will be amazed at how much easier it

will be for you to manage your finances if you train yourself to live within your means.

2. Set up a budget tracking system that works for you and keep track of your spending every single day. This will help you learn more about your spending habits and where you can make changes that will allow you to stay within your budget more easily.

3. Keep tabs on physical spaces where you deal with money. Now that the mental clutter has been taken care of, you will need to monitor the spaces that you share with money, such as your bank statements. Frequently check your balances and stay on top of your money and spending.

Stop Money Avoidance:

Are you afraid of your landlord? Do you avoid doing certain things that you know will create a backlog?

Does the mere sight of your landlord cause your palms to sweat and make your heart pound in your chest?

Let's face it: many people avoid their landlord and simply HATE to see the landlord coming. And while I agree that some landlords are certainly intimidating, *you should never be afraid of money.*

Remember, money is NOT your landlord.

It's just money.

Therefore, you should NEVER avoid money.

Instead, try to recognize why you're so afraid of it. Chances are good that you're afraid that if you get too close to it, it will run away from you or disappear. It can seem like a slippery thing — and sometimes it is, but I am here to help you catch it and hold onto it!

The truth is, the more you avoid your landlord, the worse things get. The same is true for money: if you don't think about money, put it away for retirement, or try to take care of any financial problems you have, those problems will just keep piling up — until one day it's WAY too late to do anything about it.

Oftentimes, when we think of money, we picture someone taking it away from us—demanding rent, or threatening eviction. We don't picture money as the potential solution to problems around us. But the thing is: money isn't your landlord. Money can help you fix things with your landlord (or maybe even get a nicer place!), but money isn't your landlord, and you shouldn't be afraid of it!

If you want to approach your financial situation in a new way, you should definitely join my program.

When people who are afraid of their finances think about wealth, they often envision debt and poverty. Money avoiders live with a poor money mindset and believe that they do not deserve to be wealthy. The idea of wealth may make some people uncomfortable or uneasy, but I want you to take away this idea.

You cannot make room for money if you operate in- a spirit of lack or fear.

Money avoiding behaviors such as not checking your bank account, not balancing your spending, and not setting a budget will leave you in a terrible financial position. If you are avoiding money for any of the reasons listed above, stop now!

The way to stop avoiding your finances is simple- you just have to change your mindset about what having wealth means. Wealth does not have to equal greed or being greedy, so why not start thinking of ways that money can improve your life?

You might not think so, but if you don't have a savings account, you're avoiding money. If you haven't had a steady income and are living off your credit card, you're avoiding money. And if you've been using your tax refund as an excuse to buy that new car, you're definitely avoiding money.

It's time to stop.

You can't clean up your financial house if you're not willing to take the time and energy needed to do so.

It will take a lot of hard work, but it's worth doing when you see how much more money comes into your bank account after!

Are you ready to make money your roommate, not your Landlord?

_____

_____

_____

_____

_____

_____

_____

_____

_____

_____

_____

_____

In what ways will you begin cleaning your financial house today?

What are some trash spending habits that you have, and how can you clean up your spending?

_____

_____

_____

_____

_____

_____

_____

_____

_____

_____

_____

_____

CHAPTER 2:

STOP HUSTLING BACKWARDS

Are you hustling backwards?

Most people are.

What is hustling backwards? It's when we continuously trade time for money throughout our lives. This limits our time and ability to pursue the things that are most important to us.

Over the years, I have learned that the more you can focus on building your skills and passions into a sustainable business model, then the less likely it will be that you have to trade your valuable time away to make ends meet.

The old saying, "time is more valuable than money," has never been truer. Money will always exist, but time only moves in one direction—forward. So, you must stop trading time for money if you want more of it.

Of course, you can't go back and get the hours you spent working for someone else back, but you can work smarter instead of harder to save yourself some time and make more money. The problem is that most people don't know how to get it. They've been conditioned to think that working for money can buy them happiness and freedom—but it doesn't work that way. That's why they keep trading their time for money when they should be spending their time doing the things they love with the people they love.

That's where my program, *Next Bracket for You,* comes in. I believe that everyone has a unique set of skills and passions that are valued by others. The hard part is figuring out how to package these skills into a product or service that other people need, want, and will pay for. But we teach you how to do this which in turn unlocks the door to financial freedom. *Next Bracket for You,* will help you free up your time to do the things that matter most to you. You've got the skills and we've got the opportunity. Let us do the grunt work so you can focus on what really matters! Our vetted team of coaches and students who have successfully tapped into their next bracket will help you skip to 7 or 8 figures in no time!

You see, when you are working a job, your income is limited by the hours that are available, and how much your employer thinks you deserve to make per hour. No amount of work will create more minutes. You could make more money by working harder, longer hours, but why? The ultimate goal is to work smarter, with fewer hours.

With us, you can make the most of your time and grow your earnings exponentially! My program is designed to maximize earnings from any type of job or investment. It's easy to use and easy to get started.

All you need to do is sign up and start making money!

I know that you're ready to make more money. In fact, I can almost feel you itching to get started! But before you do that, let me ask you this: how much time do you have? Are you still trading time for money and working 40 to 60 hours each week?

If you follow the steps inside of this book, money will come into your life to make life's load easier on you, just like a roommate. When I finally allowed money to move in, I instantly stopped trading time for money and started watching money make more money for me. Now, I have more time to myself than ever. I know how hard this journey may seem at first glance, but you will learn in Chapter 3 exactly how I stopped trading time for money and made a million dollars in five months.

If all your waking hours are spent doing work for somebody else, then they control what you do with every minute. Life should not be that way. You may not realize this but when you are trading time for money, your income will always be limited because no matter how many hours you put in at work or on other projects, the number of dollars coming out from each hour will remain the same. Trading away long hours for short dollars is the way that most people work, but it is time to stop hustling backward. Hustling backwards is when we continuously trade time for money throughout our lives. This limits our time and ability to pursue the things that are most important to us.

Over the years, I have learned that the more you can focus on building your skills and passions into a sustainable business model, the less likely it will be that you have to trade your valuable time away to make ends meet.

When you view money as your roommate and not your landlord, your relationship with money becomes more balanced and less stressful. When money has less control over your life, you can become more proactive with your time to create new streams that will lead you to financial advancement.

When our time is limited, our impact is limited.

It is important to remember that we should spend our time wisely and make money work for us instead. Hustling 24/7, working sunup to sundown, and working yourself to the point of exhaustion are all forms of money worshipping and ultimately lead to hustling backwards.

Money is just a tool that is meant to be used to create more money. We can always make more money but not more time.

The moment I stopped worshiping money as if it were my landlord, I started to see the true value of time and what matters most in this world.

The hustle is real.

We all have a desire to live our best lives. Providing for ourselves financially can be one of the most fulfilling achievements we set out to accomplish in life, but sometimes it feels like it is unattainable without trading in so much of our time.

"I'm so over this job. I can't do it anymore." You do not have to feel this way forever, and I am here to help you get out of what has been dragging you down for years.

Your job may feel like a death sentence rather than something fulfilling and rewarding at the end of a long day, but there are ways to take back control and start living life on your own terms again!

It may feel as if there are no other options available because the only way that seems feasible is by working endlessly with little payoff or financial security (hustling backwards). You deserve more than working 40 plus hours just to receive a paycheck for your work. You deserve more time for yourself, enjoyment, and fulfillment.

You deserve more than just 26 paychecks per year.

Let's stop trading time for money and start monetizing your downtime. To do this, you will need to create an offer that you can sell and deliver without having to work long hours.

I know what you might be thinking – "I don't have anything of value to sell!" Trust me when I say that if you want more balance in your life (and bank account), then now is the time to make this shift away from trading hours for dollars and instead focus on converting passive income.

You're on the right path.

You already want to make more money, and that's why I created *Next Bracket for You*– because if you want to achieve financial independence, then it needs to be done now. The sooner you start, the better off you'll be!

When I started my journey, I did not have plenty of people who helped me along the way. That is what inspired my program, and that's what we are here for

– to be your guide and help you get started making passive income and better financial decisions! Using money the right way will help you achieve your goals faster. It is not impossible. You just need someone who did it to show you the way. I can show you how to start building wealth and living on a budget without sacrificing all of your time or energy! With my simple strategies, anyone with an internet connection can learn how they too can achieve financial freedom today!

What does hustling backwards mean to you?

In what ways can you stop trading time for money?

If you currently have debt, how are you handling it?

CHAPTER 3:
THE TRIFECTA COMBO

After years of experimenting with different online marketing strategies, I finally found the holy grail. By authentically and honestly providing value to my audience and followers, I made one million dollars in five months immediately after I stopped trading my time for money.

And it's not just me.

In fact, there are countless students from all walks of life who have found success using my simple strategy.

If you're tired of gimmicks that don't work and are looking for a way to build a credible, profitable brand that will last for decades to come, then this is for you!

From Section 8, ex-felon, high school dropout, to being a multi-millionaire, I can tell you that E-commerce is a huge hit! I make more money in the comfort of my home in one month than what most people make in a year. The truth is that E-commerce is booming and everyone wants to get in on it. If you're not taking advantage of this opportunity, then you are missing out. Please, stop waiting for things to happen and start taking action. There is no time like the present!

Build a Product

The first thing you need to do is build a product. You can use your existing skills to build it or learn new ones if you need to. There are many resources out there that can help you develop a new skill. Remember, the internet is your friend!

Bundle it

Now that you have your product, it's time to bundle it. Make sure you're not just bundling products, but that they complement each other and fit together seamlessly! This will make your customer's experience more pleasant. Please don't just bundle any old thing - do research on what people actually want before deciding what combination of items will work best for them (and cost less than if they bought everything separately).

Sell it

Once you have built and bundled your product, it's time to sell it! This can be done through an online store. The possibilities are endless when you bundle products.

Over the years, I learned that people care more about quantity. People want to feel like they are getting a great deal for the price that they pay. So, I learned how to truly capitalize with what I call "The Trifecta Combo."

The Trifecta Combo helped me make a million dollars in five months.

Here's how:

I stopped trading my time for money and started selling products that I chose to bundle for my customers to provide them with more products for their money.

As a person who is looking for some relief from the never-ending grind, let me tell you that it does not take much effort or creativity to find products with high demand.

I offered three products to customers, and I strategically priced the bundled products at $100.

I started offering customers as many deals as possible using the Trifecta Combo so that they could take advantage of the sales without feeling guilty for spending their hard-earned cash on multiple products.

"The Trifecta Combo" is described as selling three products that equal $100 total.

When I wanted to get to my first $10,000, I knew that I only needed 100 customers to support and purchase three items bundled in my trifecta combo.

When I wanted to get to my first $100,000, I knew that I only needed 1,000 people to purchase from me using my trifecta combo.

It sounds challenging at first, but once you start to think about it differently and apply these tips that I used to make a million dollars in five months, it becomes clear that this will work for any business or product type.

If you are struggling with cash flow right now because your customers are not buying enough of one particular item alone, don't worry! With just some simple tweaks to your strategy, which include applying these principles, you will be well on your way to your first million in business.

One of the surest ways to set your brand up for long-term success is by selling a product that can easily be bundled or grouped with different products. This may sound like an intimidating task but trust me, "The Trifecta Combo" truly WORKS!

I used the *Trifecta Combo* to begin bundling products together and selling them at a discount online. Customers loved getting a bunch of great products for one low price, and I got to make passive income from them buying stuff that I chose and put together for my customers. Now I'm making over $20,000 per month from this method alone. And it's all because I decided not to trade my time for money anymore!

The Benefits of The Trifecta Combo:

Increase Your Sales

Bundling items together can help you make more sales. If customers buy one thing, they are often willing to buy more. For example, if people buy lotion by itself, they might also want to buy soap and body spray. Grouping your items makes it easier for customers to buy more than one item at a time. This helps your store by increasing the average order value.

Gain More Customers

Bundling is a great way to attract customers. Customers will buy three items that will lead them to come back for more items in the future. Customers will get additional items that they did not plan on buying at first, but once the customer sees their bundle price and how much more value they are getting from you, plus all the other cool options you have available too, they are bound to stay!

Become a Master at Merchandising

You will learn how to maximize company profits and manage the performance of each product coupled in the three-part combo. You will then be able to determine which products perform well, which bundles customers prefer, and plan promotions and markdowns as necessary.

The Trifecta Combo turned money into my roommate. I saw an instant increase in sales, and a decrease in the amount of time I invested in working.

Creating an online product is powerful because you can create it once and then focus the rest of your time on selling it. Stop trading time for money by creating a product now so that all of those hours spent working can be reduced, while your products make the money for you. If you are unsure of what products to sell, I can help you make the process seamless.

Let's put your most popular product up on sale, as well as two other high-quality items that will work perfectly together for a total price of $100.

Imagine selling to 100 customers per week? Now, you've increased your income to $10,000 per week.

I have the methods and strategies to help you sell the perfect product to the right audiences. From what I teach, The Trifecta Combo will take your business where it needs to go next. Trust me, the sooner you get started, the faster you can reach your next bracket. **Join *Next Bracket for You* today, and start your path to a better financial life tomorrow.**

Next Bracket for You **is a program that helps you manage your financial future by allowing you to do things like:**

- **Create a plan for the future**
- Better manage your checking and savings accounts
- Prepare for retirement
- Make decisions about how to invest your money

You can also get personalized answers from our team of millionaire students who will help you figure out how to get started on the best financial path. With *Next Bracket for You*, everything's in one place, and it's easy to understand.

We know that everyone's financial situation is different, so we'll guide you through all kinds of options. We'll even help you cut back on spending so you can save more money for the future.

CHAPTER 4:
HUSTLE TO THE NEXT BRACKET

I come from super humble beginnings. I worked two full-time jobs, Skechers shoe store during the day and a warehouse at night, making a total of $500 per week. I deeply needed change, so after I quit Skechers, I put my thinking cap on and began to research what business I wanted to start.

One day, I received a phone call from my sister who told me that my mom had a stroke. I told my manager about it and asked to leave work early so I could go be with my mother. The manager replied, "No, it's Saturday. Go back out there and sell some shoes." After that day, I quit Sketchers and never looked back.

In August 2018, I launched my skincare brand, Ko Elixir from my apartment. I started my skincare company and named it after my wife and I.

My goal for Ko Elixir is to provide skincare products for the everyday woman who struggles with skin problems like acne or wrinkles without breaking the bank or using harsh chemicals that can actually make your skin worse over time. Believe it or not, my top selling products are all sold using The Trifecta Combo referenced in Chapter 3.

I made one million in the first five months of opening the newly launched skincare company, and three million by the end of the first year of opening. Since then, we have made millions per month and have opened many six-figure businesses.

I made over seven figures before I turned 30 years old.

You may have thought that seven-figures were impossible, but I am here with a blueprint for you. I know that the idea of building your business to seven figures sounds like a daunting task. You may be wondering what it will take, how to do it and most importantly if you can even do it. Don't worry. I am here to tell you that with my help and guidance on these next steps of your business journey, from start to finish, we will be able to turn your seven-figure vision into reality.

I understand that the idea of turning your dreams into a reality can feel overwhelming and stressful and it is okay to feel that way. However, we need to get past those feelings and start getting excited about this journey!

It does not matter how small or large your vision is, you can do this.

I started with $300.

Now I'm a millionaire.

It's because I had a vision for what my life could be, and I was determined to make it happen, and now

I'm here because I want to give you that same opportunity: the chance to believe in yourself, to see what your life can be, and to work towards it every day.

I know that this isn't easy. It wasn't easy for me — and there were times when I wasn't sure if I could keep going, but somehow, deep within myself, I knew that if I just kept pushing forward day after day, I'd get there, and it happened.

You know what the worst feeling is? When you're working hard — day in and day out — but you have no idea where you're going. You're trapped in an endless cycle of chasing things you don't really care about and never getting anywhere meaningful with your life. It's like being on a treadmill that's speeding up faster and faster while you try desperately to keep up — but as soon as you do one thing right, five more things go wrong and suddenly, you're back at square one.

That's why I created Next Bracket for YOU: to help you figure out where you are now, and where you could go. The opportunities are endless with my program.

Are you in a financial bracket that you're satisfied with? Or do you sometimes wonder, "What would it be like to live the life of my dreams?" Do you have big ideas but need a little help bringing them to life?

I'm here to tell you that if you want more than what your current financial bracket can provide, there is no reason to settle. I know this because I used to be just like you.

Now, I am living MY dream—and helping others do the same. I started my journey at the bottom of the financial totem pole. I worked hard to get out of debt, and then I realized that I could use the lessons I learned to help other people live their dream lives too.

And that's when *Next Bracket for You* was born.

I knew many people who were struggling to make ends meet in life. I started to wonder how these people could break free from their chains and be financially free. So, that's when it hit me: Why not start a business that helps others create wealth and success?

In my program, you'll learn how to build wealth through investing in *yourself*! Once you sign up, you will receive unlimited access to training along with daily tips on how to get to your next tax bracket.

You also get an opportunity to chat with our millionaire experts in real-time. So, what are you waiting for? It's time to join the thousands of people who have ditched their 9-5 jobs and became wealthy through by joining *Next Bracket for You*.

Next Bracket for You is an online course and monthly membership site designed with one goal in mind: helping people like YOU get out of whatever financial bracket they may be in, and move up to their NEXT tax bracket. This program will teach you how to make money from wherever you are, so you can become a millionaire from your cell phone!

While most millionaire mentors simply coach you to success, I work on coaching while simultaneously giving you the products that you need to take your business to the next level. I work hard to help you scale your business, learn how it works, and create ways to make it work even better.

I use this same approach with all my students, whether you are an advanced entrepreneur or beginner. Many people join the team with no idea how to get started, limited access to capital, and no products.

In my program, I strategically show students how to successfully start and grow any business in any industry, so that my students can also leave a legacy behind for their families.

My program is for everyone, no matter if you have a business or not. I turned my small business into an eight-figure empire, and so can you.

Together, we can make a plan for moving forward financially with no more worry about bills or financial obligations.

Next Bracket 4 U has classes in every city, all around the country. If you are not living your best life financially because of bills and financial obligations, it is time to take charge!

Next Bracket 4 U has helped people just like you create a plan for moving forward without worrying about money or finances so that they can live their best lives. Maybe you've spent years paying down your credit card debt, and now you're ready to start investing in your future. Or maybe you're finally ready to make the leap from renting to buying a home.

If you're like many of our students, all this talk of buying mansions, obtaining mortgages, and investment opportunities feels like a foreign language — one you don't have time to learn.

Our financial team at Next Bracket 4 U is here to help you bridge the gap between where you are now and where you want to be in your personal finances. We do it by helping you:

- Create a budget that helps reduce your stress, not add to it
- Maximize income so that you can afford the things that matter most
- Find the right products for your unique needs

We know that financial decisions are some of the hardest choices we will ever make; but we also know that these decisions don't have to be made alone. Our mission is to work with clients on every step of their journey so they can reach their goals without worrying about finances!

Next Bracket 4 U has helped people just like you create a plan for moving forward without worrying about money or finances so that they can live and be their best.

You deserve this too!

If you have not attended a *Next Bracket for You* class, you should. Our classes will truly change your life.

Choose from three program options:

Option 1: $40 monthly membership

Option 2: $5,000 annual membership

Option 3: $30,0000 business in a box accelerated membership where everything is done for you to help you skip to your next bracket.

Learn how to pay down your debts, save for emergencies, invest, and reduce expenses where possible without sacrificing necessary living costs like food or shelter. Join the program by visiting www.nextbracket4u.com for more details.

Your next bracket is ready for you!

Write a plan below to get to your next bracket.

What will life look like when you get to your next bracket? Visualize your next bracket and develop a plan of action to get to it.

_____

_____

_____

_____

_____

_____

_____

_____

_____

_____

CHAPTER 5:

NEVER LET YOUR ROOMMATES COME EMPTY-HANDED

There's a new roommate who just moved into your place—and his name is Money. You might be thinking: "Money? My new roommate?!"

But hear me out.

Money is a great roommate, as long as he doesn't have any bad habits. That's why I want to tell you a little bit about what to expect from Money so that he can be a great housemate for years to come (if you decide to keep him around).

One thing about Money is that he is always on the move. He never stays in one place for too long, which means he won't always be at home with you. This might sound like a bad thing, but it just means that you have to make sure Money is upholding his part of the bills, exceedingly and abundantly.

Money can be very valuable.

You might think that having an extra person around the house will mean more expenses and less room for you and your stuff, but keep in mind that Money is here to HELP you.

Your new roommate (Money) should never be two things: lazy or empty-handed.

What I mean by this is, do not start businesses that do not guarantee a return on your investment. Do not invite any roommates who do not help pay the bills, are always short on rent, and are plain old lazy.

Do not spend money on things that are not working for you. Money needs to keep making money for you.

Your business and money should be able to withstand any financial obstacle. If you have a business that is not making a return or is not paying its half of the rent, you may have a lazy roommate in your life.

Lazy roommates do not produce anything.

Lazy roommates are those business investments that make empty promises to make you money but have no proven path or knowledge to do so. You wouldn't invest in a lazy roommate, so why would you invest in a lazy business?

Having this sort of roommate around for too long will cause you to remain in debt, so it is important to take out the trash on a lazy roommate (or business) early.

Bad investments will only deplete your money! So, only make room for good investments. You can do this by recognizing when an investment is not working out and immediately cutting it loose.

I help students find low-cost start-up products so that they do not have to think about how to obtain products too much. I am all about empowering up and coming entrepreneurs with the tools they need to succeed because I know what it's like to be one of them.

The financial literacy programs that I offer are the exact opposite of lazy roommates. I teach students how to live with more than enough income from passive sources.

I have a team with a proven track record that will show you exactly how we've helped other businesses skyrocket their profit margins, and we can show you how we'll do the same for yours. We can prove to you that our knowledge is legitimate, and that we have a clear path for helping you reach your goals.

We don't just *talk* about making money—we actually get up off the couch and do it (and at times, we don't even leave the couch to make money).

We are far from lazy roommates. It's time to say goodbye to roommates that do not bring you a return on your investment.

Your 9 to 5 has ceilings, but Entrepreneurship has no limits.

If you normally get paid twice a month, Entrepreneurship can increase it to double, triple, or more of that amount per month. Let's say your average check is $1,000 every two weeks. You can take $200 to

$300 out of that check to invest in the *Next Bracket 4 U* program that is guaranteed to show you how to get products for low and resell products at a much higher price.

I will help you create a brand, order your initial products, and label your products through the avenues that I provide for you. I will help you turn money into your roommate and multiply your monthly revenue.

With the right investments, you can make money work for you.

This means that you should take your time to research what kind of investment is best for your needs, and then invest accordingly. Do not just jump into a business model because it sounds good without fully understanding how or why it works. If you need help choosing a type of investment, I am happy to help you find an option that suits your financial situation and goals.

You need to be able to make your money work for you so that it keeps making more. If your business isn't paying its half of the rent or if it is just not producing anything, then allow me to help you get rid of these lazy money-making habits now before they ruin everything!

I do not allow my students to live with lazy money roommates. If their businesses are not making them money, I give my students the tools to take their businesses to new heights.

I have been teaching students how to sell online for three years now, and I can tell you that it is possible to do 50 million per year in sales if you know what you are doing.

My program will teach you everything that I know about selling online so that your business can grow as fast as possible! The most money in the world these days is happening by selling online products through E- commerce.

I have a couple of friends who are making 50 to 100 million per year using strategies that they learned from my program. I have million-dollar days without ever having to leave my home. The goal is to always have full control over money, without ever worshipping money.

I simply do not allow lazy roommates to enter into my life. As for you, if your roommate (money) is being lazy and not paying rent, it's okay to kick him out, or start a new business venture that is *guaranteed* to bring a return on your investment.

Of course, if you don't manage your money or investments properly, you could get evicted — which means you'd have to start over from scratch. I am here to help you avoid any money traps that could cause your business to plummet.

If your business does not bring a return on your investment, then you, my friend, have an empty-handed roommate. No worries, though! I can help you fix that. Our team at Next Bracket for You will get to work evaluating your business's sales strategies and pipeline so that you can see maximum profits. Get in touch with us today!

CHAPTER 6:
AVOID EVICTION

No matter how much money you make, you must avoid self-inflicted wounds that are caused by the misuse of money. Misusing money happens when we overspend. It happens when we buy cars that we cannot afford, homes we cannot afford, and increase our cost of living while paying for it with debt.

Misusing money is sure to lead to eviction, foreclosure, bankruptcy, repossession, unfulfilled dreams, and a life of financial stress.

Being financially successful is more than just being able to pay your bills on time. Being financially successful means being able to take care of your family in times of need. It means being able to retire comfortable. It means having the financial freedom to live life the way you want to live it.

I've been helping people on their journey to financial success since I quit Sketchers. I have helped thousands of people find financial success through seminars and coaching programs, and I've learned that misusing money happens mostly for those who continue to treat money like it's their landlord.

Eventually, their landlord (money) will kick them out for not being able to pay on time. To avoid eviction, put your money into investments that will not allow you to go back to ground zero.

Do not allow your money to get back into that landlord position in your life. Always remember, you can bring in more roommates to help you. Having more roommates come into your life will help you take back control and become the Lord of the land.

Furthermore, do not give away money just as quickly as you get it. Instead, reinvest back into your business to make it flourish later. Putting money in its place helps you understand that money is not about the *now*.

Money is about the latter. Release the *false sense of urgency of money* that you base your whole life around.

You should not treat your money with scarcity.

When you look at money differently, you will save money differently. Having money as your roommate will get you out of different situations. The goal is to have so many roommates that you can take back full control, and you will not have to rent anymore.

Think about it! If you get too many roommates in your apartment, you then upgrade to your dream house and take ownership of the land.

You can truly create generational wealth using the money methods that I teach. If you are looking to make your money work for you, there are plenty of ways that I can help you do so. I enjoy empowering people who are ready to take control of their finances.

Avoid eviction by investing your time and energy into projects that will bring in more income. I have been in the business of helping people with their finances since launching my *Next Bracket 4 U* program. Last year, I created 26 millionaires in my program. I provide insight on how to turn your money around so that you can use the money for more than paying bills, and invest in your future.

If you want to make your money work for you instead of against you, then let's identify what may be going wrong in your financial life and get started fixing it.

What are the biggest obstacles that keep you from getting ahead financially?

_____

_____

_____

_____

_____

_____

_____

_____

_____

_____

_____

In what ways can you overcome those financial hurdles?

CHAPTER 7:

MARKET TO YOUR FIRST MILLION

During my time working with many entrepreneurs and helping them build their businesses, I learned the best marketing strategies that have allowed me to make the most of my time and money.

When I initially started, I used my last $300 Sketchers check and spent $200 on products and $100 on marketing. Once I created a solid plan for my method of selling products, my business took me to the next level.

Networking is key.

I was able to find the perfect social media groups for me to start marketing and promoting my products. I created a business page, and I shared it inside of private Facebook groups to start building hype around my new products. After building hype on my business page, I searched for followers who would buy my products once I released them.

I found two influencers and I paid them to market my product. I requested for them to share and repost my product, and I gained followers from each influencer.

From my business page, I sent a direct message to every person that followed me, and I made myself a discount code just to say welcome to the page, as well as to make a return on sales.

Today, I have made 8 figures in less than 3 years with these same practices. I stayed humble, stayed down, and I made money work for me. There was no way that I could have made my first million without knowing that money does not have the power to control me. I learned how to take my power back from money. I learned to never be afraid of money.

Becoming a self-made millionaire is not as difficult a journey as many would imagine. In addition, building a seven-figure business is well within reach for nearly any business owner who is open to learning, growing, and applying the necessary pressure for their business.

Today, I provide business owners with access to information, tools, and strategies necessary to further build their brands. I enjoy helping students create their blueprints to get to their first million.

I know what it takes to be successful and how hard it can be without proper guidance. When I first started marketing my business, I had to learn how to observe, listen, and identify the needs of customers.

Money is only a by-product of value creation. To earn money in business, do not focus on the money itself, but rather focus on growing it to increase value.

The more you chase money, the more it will run away from you. The only way for money to follow

you is by making money be your helpmate. Money is easy to move around, and investing money into things that bring value to your business makes it possible to reach your next bracket. Use the money to accumulate more money. I was eager to get out of the landlord mindset and become the Lord of the land. My goal was to own everything. And that is what I did. I marketed my products to my first million dollars because I truly realized that I was in control of money and marketing.

Having a solid strategy for your business will change your life. It has changed mine and it has done the same for dozens of my clients and students who have hired me to help them make their first million. The goal is to optimize your business so you can make more money than you are making now while reducing the time you spend working.

Your money should always work for you, but between fees, interest rates, and a bunch of other financial jargon that can make your head spin, it's hard to know how to get the most out of money.

That's where joining my program comes in. We'll teach you how to save your money the smart way, so you can not only feel more secure about your financial future, but also be able to do more with what you've got today. It's all about keeping more of what's yours in your pocket and less in the pockets of banks and credit card companies.

Sign up TODAY to start learning how!

CHAPTER 8:
READY, SET, LAUNCH!

It can be hard to feel like you're getting anywhere in life when it comes to finances, but it's important to know that the financial position you are in now is not the position you will be in forever. It's not *completely* your fault that you are where you are! Many people make a lot of bad financial decisions simply because they don't have the right information. You can only make good decisions if you have the right information.

Now that you have the right information, what are you going to make your money do for you?

I have given you some strategies on how to clean up your financial house, so now it is time for you to get started. It will be worth every minute if you want a better life financially.

Money is just a tool for getting what you want.

Money is your partner, not an idol for you to worship. If money becomes your idol or something to worship, then you should stop and take the time to figure out what you truly value in life. You work hard, and that's fantastic, but what if you could work less hard, and earn even more?

It turns out your money mindset can shape how much you earn, as well as how much you're able to enjoy it when you have it. If you're always worried about having more money, or if you don't feel like you're earning enough—and you let those fears shape how you view money—you might not be as effective at earning money as you would be otherwise. But if you're able to change your mindset so that you focus on earning enough to meet your needs and then savor the good feelings of having done so, you'll earn more per hour than someone who's just trying to earn as much as possible through hard work.

People's mindsets and their relationship to their finances are revealed through their spending habits. People who have a growth mindset about money tend to earn more than those with a fixed money mindset.

Expand your mind to expand your money.

Money can be used as an important resource, but if you put too much importance on working harder for more and more money, you will not be able to live a fulfilling life. A life of hard work does not have to be your only choice. Whether you are a student, an employee, or a business owner, there is always more that you could do to have the life you've always dreamed of.

But what does that mean?

What does it mean to have the life you've always dreamed of?

It means having more time for your family, traveling anywhere in the world, and making a difference in your community. It means living a fulfilling life — a life where every day is an opportunity to learn something and contribute to what matters most to you.

How do you get that kind of life? You don't have to work any harder than you already are. You just need the right tools. Allow this book to be an assessment tool that helps you understand how to stop worshipping money and take charge of your very own financial situation today. Always view money as a roommate, because money is here to help you by paying half of your expenses. Allow your new roommate (money) to help you live your life with less stress, more fun, and better health.

Like any good roommate, you will be grateful when more money comes into your home because of all the ways it will help you out!

So, what are you waiting for?

Visit www.nextbracket4u.com for more information on how to take control of your financial future.

ABOUT THE AUTHOR

Keenan Williams became a self-made millionaire with only 300 bucks using every method outlined inside of this book. Williams started with humble beginnings, working around the clock to make ends meet.

Williams has a very inspirational story that can serve as a motivation to us all. Before entrepreneurship, Williams hustled 24/7, working to support his newborn daughter. In the 11th grade, Keenan dropped out of high school and took on two full-time jobs to provide for his family.

One day, Williams received a phone call from his sister who told him that his mom had a stroke. Williams told his manager about it and asked to leave work early so he could go be with his mother.

His manager replied, "No, it's Saturday. Go back out there and sell some shoes." After that day, Keenan quit and never looked back.

In August 2018, Williams launched his skincare brand, Ko Elixir from his apartment. In the beginning, it was a little doubtful as he struggled with trusting himself and his decisions. After developing a tactical marketing plan and receiving positive customer feedback, 6 months later, Keenan Williams became a huge success. Since launching, Ko Elixir has resulted in impressive success. However, the path to entrepreneurship was not an easy road for Williams.

Due to his highly impressive success, Williams launched a monthly program to teach members the step-by-step process he used in business and marketing. Williams is the author of *Money is Not Your Landlord, Money is Your Roommate,* and he desires to help the world put money in its rightful place.

Williams faced a lot of troubles to stand where he is today. He used his knowledge wisely and created a business from the ground up. He accumulated knowledge from every place he worked and then applied the knowledge to become a millionaire. It's evident from Keenan Williams's life that you can achieve anything if you are determined and willing to work smart.

DISCLAIMER

Legal Disclosure: You are hereby advised that Keenan Williams is not a financial advisor and is NOT providing legal or tax advice. Nothing in this book or its attachments should be interpreted by you as legal advice. For legal advice and all legal related matters, Keenan Williams recommends that you seek the advice of a qualified attorney licensed in your state or jurisdiction. All rights reserved. No part of this publication may be reproduced, distributed, or transmitted in any form or by any means, including photocopying, recording, or other electronic or mechanical methods, without the prior written permission of the publisher, except in the case of brief quotations embodied in critical reviews and certain other noncommercial uses permitted by copyright law.

www.ingramcontent.com/pod-product-compliance
Lightning Source LLC
Chambersburg PA
CBHW070733230426
43665CB00035B/2238